Helping Children to Speak Clearly and Confidently

A guide for parents, teachers and children of all ages

It is never too early or too late to learn to speak clearly and confidently

How would your children benefit if you help them to speak clearly?

1. Children who can speak clearly and confidently are happy children.

2. Children who can speak clearly and confidently are more likely to be top of their class because they're not frightened to speak or ask the teacher questions.

3. Children who can speak clearly and confidently are willing to join in social events - parties, clubs, sports etc. They don't need to have a parent with them all the time because they can speak for themselves. You, as a parent don't need to worry if they'll ask to use the toilet etc.

4. Children who can speak clearly and confidently are successful children.

5. Confident, successful children sleep well at night.

Copyright © Serena Greenslade 2011

www.Afraid-of-speaking-a-speech.com

serena@afraid-of-speaking-a-speech.com

Contents

Articulation	5
Organs of speech	6
Vowel Sounds	6
Consonant Sounds	8
Exercise and Drills	9
Breathing	13
Expressive Speech	16
Inflection	16
Pause	16
Pace	17
Pitch	18
Power	19
Resonance	19
Facial Expression	20
Reading Aloud	21
National Curriculum	22
5 Steps to preparing a speech	23
5 Steps to practising a speech	24
Open your mouth	25
3 steps to slowing down	26
5 steps to standing correctly	28
10 Top Tips	29
Topics for talks	30
Poems for children to speak aloud	32
Voice Exercises	35
Bonus Lesson for Young Children	38
Bonus Lessons for Older Children	55

Even in this age of emails, text messaging and social networking the spoken word is still the most effective way of communicating and to succeed in the world today, children and adults need to be able to communicate with confidence.

The way we talk influences the way other people think of us and consequently how they react to us.

As parents we don't hesitate to teach our children to count – we're always asking 'how many?' Most of us can't resist trying to teach our children to read before they start school but how many of us teach our children to speak? We assume that they'll pick it up just by listening to us, however some children need a little help along the way.

ARTICULATION

Articulation is the art of speaking and involves the study of the muscles we use for speech. Good articulation has three advantages.

1. It enables us to speak for long periods of time without tiring. As in any activity, muscles used correctly can work more effectively for much longer than muscles used incorrectly.

2. The more these muscles are exercised, the clearer the speech becomes and listeners find it much easier to understand you. As in sport, the fitter you are the easier it becomes.

3. It enables you and the audience to concentrate more on the content of what you're saying rather than how you're saying it, they don't need to decipher it.

LAZINESS
Many problems of articulation are caused by bad habits and laziness. We may mumble our words or perhaps speak out of the corner of our mouth because we want to sound like our friends, it might not be fashionable to speak clearly. However, most cases of bad articulation are caused by laziness. We know what we are saying so we expect other people to know what we mean. We just can't be bothered to use our mouths. There is no reason why people should know in advance what you are going to say, therefore you must speak clearly and use your facial muscles to produce good clear speech.

TOP TIP
Over precise speech is as bad as lazy speech.

ORGANS OF SPEECH

There are five organs of speech:

The tongue

The lips

The teeth

The hard palate

The soft palate

As the sound enters the mouth these organs of speech alter the sound.

The tongue is the only muscle in the body connected directly to a bone, it can move in and out, from side to side, it can twist and can move very quickly.

The lips can be moved forwards and backwards and can change the shape of the mouth

The teeth cannot move but are used in conjunction with the lips and tongue. We notice the importance of teeth when we listen to young children who are waiting for the tooth fairy to arrive or to more elderly people whose teeth have unfortunately not managed to reach such an old age as they have!

The soft palate is the back of the roof of the mouth. It can be lowered or raised for differing sounds.

The hard palate is the front of the roof of the mouth and can't move. It is the bony bit near the teeth and like the teeth it's used in conjunction with the tongue.

Try saying these two simple words: AT ALL

These two little words represent four sounds and the tongue moves so quickly to produce these four sounds that we don't realize. We have 'a' as in cat, 't' as in tuh, 'aw' as in crawl and 'l' in luh.

VOWEL SOUNDS

Speech sounds are either vowel sounds or consonant sounds. We have five vowels, a, e, i, o and u but as many as twenty six different vowel sounds.

For example take the vowel 'a' now imagine its sound in the following words, car, cat and way.

Now do the same with the 'e' sound in 'bet' and 'bee'.

Each sound is different and it's the sound that's important not the name of the letter. The breath of vowel sounds comes up through the vocal cords and straight out through the mouth. The different sounds are made by altering the positions of the tongue and lips. Note that for vowel sounds the organs of speech never touch each other. The teeth shouldn't touch the lips, the tongue shouldn't touch the hard palate and the lips shouldn't touch each other. Sometimes the tongue might rest behind the bottom teeth although technically it shouldn't.

MORE TECHNICAL DETAILS

For those of you who might be interested in more technical details there are three types of vowel sounds. If the position of the lips and tongue do not alter during the sound it's a monophthong. An example is 'ee'. Once the sound has been started the mouth stays in the same position. There are open and shut (or long and short) monophthongs.

SHUT – Th<u>a</u>t p<u>e</u>n <u>i</u>s n<u>o</u>t m<u>u</u>ch g<u>oo</u>d. Remember it is the vowel sound that you need that has been underlined.

OPEN – H<u>ea</u>t s<u>oo</u>n f<u>or</u>ms f<u>ir</u>m pl<u>a</u>nts

If the position of the lips and tongue alter from one position to another, the sound is a diphthong. An example is the sound 'ay'. The mouth closes slightly as you say the sound.

There are four main diphthongs and two vanish diphthongs.

The four main ones are (remember it's the sound only)

M<u>y</u> h<u>ou</u>se j<u>oi</u>ns n<u>ew</u>

The two vanish ones are: r<u>oa</u>d w<u>ay</u>

So the sentence for remembering diphthongs is 'my house joins new road way'.

If there are three positions the sound is a triphthong. An example of this is 'our' which is often mispronounced as 'are' which is only a monophthong.

Triphthong sounds are fire, coir, flower and pure.

We also have neutral vowels, which are small sounds often squashed between two consonants. Examples are woman, camel, etc. They are unstressed sounds. A child learning to read stresses every sound equally so they would say 'cam mell'.

Look in the mirror you say the above words so that you can see how your mouth moves from one position to another.

TOP TIP

Say 'the' before a consonant sound i.e. 'the' bath but say 'thee' before a vowel sound, so 'the apple' is pronounced 'thee apple'.

CONSONANT SOUNDS

A consonant sound comes up through the vocal cords and is then stopped in the mouth by the contact of two of the organs of speech. We have to remember that it's the sound of the consonant and not the letter name that is important. The fourth letter of the alphabet is called 'dee' but its sound is not dee but more of a 'duh'.

To achieve good articulation each word must be finished right to the last syllable and to the final consonant. This articulation helps us to project out voice and this means that we do not have to shout which is obviously beneficial to us. Being able to use our organs of speech correctly enables the sound to carry further, just as using the correct grip will make hitting a tennis or golf ball a lot easier and will enable it to go further. The wrong technique in sport will give you aches and pains and shouting or whispering in speech will hurt your throat.

The organs of speech need as much training and care as any other muscles in the body.

Try the sounds below out loud to see how the organs of speech work.

The two lips touching produce the 'p', 'b' and 'm' sounds – (puh, buh and muh) The teeth and lips touching create an 'f' or 'v' sound.

The tongue and hard palate make a 'd', 't', 'n' or 'l' sound. The tongue and soft palate produce the 'k' and 'g' sounds.

If we try to make our speech too perfect it sounds terrible and false so these end consonants need to be subtle. As long as your tongue touches the roof of your mouth you will automatically make the sound.

EXERCISE AND DRILLS

In order to improve lazy speech we have to practice and make our organs of speech work effectively. In any sport there are drills which you perform in practice over and over again but that you wouldn't dream of reproducing in a match. Dribbling around cones in football and stretching in dancing are all examples of routine drills which have to be performed daily but you wouldn't see any of the Manchester United players running around cones during a match at Old Trafford. It goes without saying that there is no point in doing any of these drills if you don't give 100%.

The same is true of speech drills. There is no point in whispering them or speaking quickly so that you can get them finished in a hurry! They have to be performed out loud and slowly if they are to do any good. Incidentally, I would never expect you to do any of these drills in public, this is because when you do these drills you must open your mouth as wide as possible which if done correctly will result in you making funny faces.

Try to speak to an object when you do these drills, it doesn't matter what it is. It could be a chair, a teddy bear, a clock or a telephone. Focus on an object – look at it and direct the sound towards that object.

Below are two different drills for vowel sounds. Make sure they are repeated out loud.

The 'I' sound pronounced 'eye'.

I tried to buy a kite last night.

Open you mouth as wide as it will go for the 'eye' sound. Pull your jaw down with your hand.

The 'o' sound pronounced 'oh'

Oh dear oh, my cake is all dough.

For the 'oh' sound you need a round mouth.

Two consonant exercises

'Ch' and 'J'

A lot of children have trouble with these two sounds. A good way to get the child to articulate these correctly is to make sure they their tongue touches the roof of their mouth before they start the sound (as in 't')

Charlie chooses chips, cheese and jam.

End Consonants

You must make sure that you sound the first and last consonant in each word. It's a bit like shouting at a child or a dog!

I lost my cat, he hid in my hat.

The last bit of dirt has just been cleaned up.

OPEN YOUR MOUTH

If you want to kick a ball you move your leg, if you want to throw a ball you move your arm and if you want to speak you must move your mouth. The sound cannot come out of a closed mouth.

Try the following sentence with your mouth shut.

'Throw the ball high in the sky'.

You might achieve a humming sound which goes up and down in pitch, it might even be a loud humming sound but no one will understand what you're trying to say because there will be no clear words.

Now say the sentence but open your mouth as wide as you can. I can guarantee it sounded better but I bet you didn't open your mouth as wide as you thought you did. Go and get a mirror and say the same sentence for a third time. This time physically pull your chin down with your hand on the 'high' and 'sky' words and make sure you make a circle with your mouth on the 'throw' word.

Obviously when you're talking in front of people there is no need to be this extreme but this is how you should practice. As we get older we are often too embarrassed to open our mouths because we think we look stupid. However, as with all muscles in our body, the mouth (lips and tongue in particular) need to be exercised.

We owe it to ourselves to look after our organs of speech with as much care as we look after other parts of our body. There are voice exercises that exercise specific muscles in the face but the easiest way to exercise is to make funny faces. Stretch the lips and tongue as much as possible and see how far you can stick your tongue out. (By the way these face exercises also help us to stay younger looking for longer!)

Try saying this sentence out loud.

'My kite is flying high in the sky'

Every 'eye' sound needs an open mouth. With your mouth open on the 'eye' sound you should be able to fit your three middle fingers in your mouth vertically. Once the muscles have been exercised it will be easier to sound the final consonants in the words. The improvement in articulation enables your voice to be heard without the need for shouting and has the added benefit of slowing your speech down. Bad articulation is usually caused by lazy muscles.

CORRECT NUMBER OF SYLLABLES

We need to be very careful not to cut words short. Quite often we're such a hurry to finish what we're saying that we miss out parts of words. Examples of this can be seen in the following words:

'Secretary' which is often shortened to 'secretry'. Instead of giving it four syllables it's only got three.

'Extraordinary' is pronounced 'extrodinary'.

'Different' is often shortened to 'diffrent'

'Every' is shortened to 'Evry'

The 'e' that is often missing in different and every only needs to be a small unstressed sound.

Some people also add syllables when they shouldn't be there. The word 'athlete' is often pronounced 'athelete'

'umbrella' is pronounced 'umberella'

'toddler' as 'toddeler'.

BREATHING

Correct breathing is essential for good speech. Every sound we make needs breath. I'm going to ask you to stand up.

Now say out loud: 'I am a brilliant coach and I'm bound to produce some champions.'

What did you do immediately before you spoke?

I would imagine that most of you pulled your shoulders up as you took a deep breath.

Lifting up your shoulders did you no good whatsoever! All you did was restrict yourself and tense your muscles. This is called clavicle breathing. With this type of breathing you are trying to move parts of the body which don't move, in particular the top ribs.

When we are asleep or resting the air enters our body slowly and escapes quickly. When speaking we need to inhale quickly and quietly. The emphasis here is on must quietly.

It must be done naturally with no preparation – you mustn't think 'now I'm going to take a breath'. If you lift your shoulders and think, ready, steady, go – there will be a gasping sound.

Breathe in through your nose as this will protect your vocal cords. Breathing through your mouth will dry out your vocal cords so it is essential that anyone with a sore throat breathes through the nose.

Good breath control is essential for good speech but it must appear natural. In order to breathe to speak we need to use our intercostal muscles and our diaphragm.

The intercostal muscles move the ribs and the diaphragm forms the bottom of the thorax and the top of the abdomen. At the centre of the diaphragm is the central tendon which joins the lower ribs, the sternum and the spine. During normal breathing the diaphragm descends about 1 cm but during strenuous breathing it can descend as much as 10 cms. Between the ribs are the external intercostals muscles and when these contract they elevate the ribs.

When we breathe in our lungs need to fill up with air. This requires our ribs to move outwards and sideways. If you place your hands on your ribs just above your waist and breathe in you should be able to feel your ribs move outwards.

As the lungs fill with air the diaphragm will move downwards, giving plenty of space for the lungs to expand. As the air is used up the diaphragm returns to its normal position – pushing the air out.

During normal breathing out (exhalation) the muscles are relaxing. The diaphragm and the external intercostals muscles relax causing the ribs to depress. Other muscles become active only after forceful breathing, as in sport or trained speaking - the abdominal muscles and the internal intercostals contract. This is a skill which has to be practiced, it does not come naturally.

It is also important that your posture is correct. Stand up and sit down again. How many of you sat down and then let your ribs drop down a second time?

We have 12 pairs of ribs. Ribs 1-7 are fixed and cannot move, consequently lifting up your shoulders or any other movement around the neck and shoulders cannot increase the size of your thorax. Ribs 8-10 can move outwards and these are the ribs we concentrate on. Ribs 11 and 12 are floating ribs and when we sit down badly, we rest the top half of our body on these ribs. Your lungs need room to expand.

I'm going to be a nuisance and ask you to stand up again.

This time imagine you are talking to a group of adults. How are your knees? Have you locked them tight?

If so, bend them a little and relax the muscles. The tension in the back of your knees will travel up your back into your neck and shoulders making breathing more difficult. Let your feet take your weight, not your knees. Stand evenly on the heels of your feet. Make sure you are not standing to attention. The only people who do this successfully are people who don't need to speak such as soldiers on parade, gymnasts and ballerinas. If you stand upright with your head up (but still relaxed and not to attention) people will immediately take notice of you. You will look as though you know what you are talking about.

Standing and sitting correctly will also make you feel less tired so you will sound much more alert.

Whilst you are sitting or standing correctly, try the following sentence. Start each line with a new breath and see how far you can get until you run out or breath (ignore punctuation)

1. I can name

2. I can name seventeen different sports

3. I can name seventeen different sports: football, baseball, cricket

4. I can name seventeen different sports: football, baseball, cricket, tennis, golf, swimming

5. I can name seventeen different sports: football, baseball, cricket, tennis, golf, swimming, boxing, squash, badminton.

6. I can name seventeen different sports: football, baseball, cricket, tennis, golf, swimming, boxing, squash, badminton, gymnastics, trampolining.

7. I can name seventeen different sports: football, baseball, cricket, tennis, golf, swimming, boxing, squash, badminton, gymnastics, trampolining, diving

8. I can name seventeen different sports: football, baseball, cricket, tennis, golf, swimming, boxing, squash, badminton, gymnastics, trampolining, diving, skiing, hockey

9. I can name seventeen different sports: football, baseball, cricket, tennis, golf, swimming, boxing, squash, badminton, gymnastics, trampolining, diving, skiing, hockey, basketball and

10. I can name seventeen different sports: football, baseball, cricket, tennis, golf, swimming, boxing, squash, badminton, gymnastics, trampolining, diving, skiing, hockey, basketball, snooker and athletics.

Although breath control is very important, we mustn't become so obsessed with taking deep breaths that we are too frightened to pause in the middle of a sentence if it makes sense to do so. Good breath control means that we can pause when we want to rather than when we have to.

EXPRESSIVE SPEECH

Once we've improved our articulation we need to make our speech sound interesting and expressive.

WORD PICTURES

Words create images in our minds. If I were to say 'Wimbledon Champion' to a group of people, they would all get pictures in their minds. These pictures would all be different and as talkers we need to be able to share these ideas. You need to be able to pick out the most important words and then make these words stand out. Therefore, the first rule of good speech is to be able to pick out the words which are important. If you are explaining to a child how to tie a shoe lace or how to brush your teeth you should instinctively know which words are important.

If you find this difficult, imagine you can only hear part of the sentence. Which words would you need to hear to be able to guess what the sentence meant? Once you know which words are important you need to be able to emphasize these words.

They need to stand out and there are various techniques for doing this.

INFLECTION

The first technique is the use of inflection. This put simply is the bending of the voice. The word may start on a lower note than it finishes the word. If you speak without using inflection the voice becomes very monotonous and people listening will fall asleep! When we ask a question we bend the voice in an upwards direction. When we have finished a thought we end on a downhill inflection.

If you want to sound passionate about your subject you will need to use inflection. A voice that has no melody sounds as thought it has no energy.

PAUSE

The main criticism of anyone speaking in public is that they tend to speak too quickly. Most of us need to slow down and make better use of the pause. Pausing helps you by giving you the chance to take a breath and think about what you're going to say next.

In any sport, once a point or goal has been scored, play stops, the player takes a breath and the spectators have a chance to acknowledge the fantastic shot or goal by clapping and cheering. Pausing during speech gives us a chance to take a breath and gives the audience time to digest what you have just said – they may even want to laugh or groan.

Pausing also helps us to emphasize important words. By pausing before an important word, you are leaving the audience in suspense – trying to guess what you're about to say next. If you pause after an important word, you give the audience a chance to reflect on what you have said – you are giving it time to sink in.

Pausing before and after an important word gives the audience a chance to do both! While you're pausing the audience has a chance to think, 'Oh yes, I see what he means', and if you say something funny they might laugh.

PACE

Pace is the speed at which you speak.

If you want to inject a feeling of excitement or anger, speed up just a little and raise the pitch of your voice. More serious topics should be approached more slowly and with a lower pitch. It is worth remembering that the larger the venue, the slower you will need to speak. Imagine your words traveling to the back of the hall, you need to open your mouth wide and give the words time to reach the people in the back row.

The same is true if you're talking to an elderly or slightly hard of hearing audience. If you're talking to an audience who are not experts in your field, for example, if you're talking about tennis (lobs, spins, different grips etc.) to an audience who aren't very familiar with these terms, you'll need to slow down slightly to give them a chance to take in what you've said. Talking outside need to be slower than talking inside especially if the weather conditions are bad as the wind and rain will swallow up your words.

The audience to not have the advantage of knowing your line of thought, therefore they cannot easily anticipate what you're going to say. If you want to share your images you will have to give them time to hear your words. We should always try to vary the pace at which we speak, someone who speaks slowly all the time is just as hard to listen to as someone who speaks quickly all the time. Think about what you are saying and alter the speed accordingly. If you speak too quickly you'll give the impression that you feel you don't deserve to be listened to and that you want to get your words out as quickly as possible before anyone notices!

All speech needs to sound fluent, and one way of making your speech sound fluent, even when you're terrified is to speed up on the small unimportant words, such as 'is', 'it' and 'the', and take more care with larger more important key words. A child learning to read gives every word the same time value.

'The cat sat on the mat' is read as six equal words. Children do not anticipate what the next word is, so they give every word the same length. Adults tend to do this if they're sight reading. How often have you heard people start a sentence and then stop and restart it when they suddenly realize what the sentence is supposed to mean?

Up until that point they have taken every word at face value. Going back to the sentence 'the cat sat on the mat', an adult might group the words as follows: 'the cat / sat / on the / mat.'

The first 'the' is unimportant, 'cat' is important, 'sat' is important, 'on the' can be run in together and 'mat' is important.

Although I wouldn't recommend that anybody should speak too quickly, there are times when you will need to be slightly faster than others. This would happen if you wanted to convey excitement, anger or a crisis of any description. You can't expect your listeners to get excites about what you're saying if you don't sound excited yourself.

PITCH

Most nervous people speak with a high pitch (as do angry people). By lowering the pitch of your voice you'll sound more confident. However, if you want to sound excited and enthusiastic as well you'll need to raise the pitch a little. Talking in a low pitch does make you sound very professional but it can also become monotonous and boring.

If you have a naturally high, squeaky voice just try lowering it a little, It's a fact that high pitched voices are harder to listen to than lower pitched voices, so to make your voice sound interesting you should only raise your voice on the important (or exciting) words.

Read the following sentence to yourself.

'It was a fantastic goal'.

Now say it out loud – twice. The first time say the word 'fantastic' lower than the other words in the sentence and the second time say the word 'fantastic' higher than the other words. Which sounded the most enthusiastic? If done properly it would have been the second.

POWER

Power is simply the volume you use. The more people you're talking to, the louder you need to speak. If you speak clearly, you will be heard more easily even if you speak quietly. Variety is the key here, if you want to sound exciting, the voice needs to be louder. If you speak too quietly you'll also give the impression that you're too frightened to be loud and that you don't want to be noticed. Confident people usually speak quite loudly because they're not afraid of the sound of their own voice and they know that what they have to say is interesting.

Remember that your voice must always be loud enough to be heard. It's very difficult to get excited about what's being said if you have to strain your ears to hear it.

RESONANCE

In order to fill a large space with sound you must learn to use your resonators. These resonators are all the hollow spaces above the larynx. The sound vibrates against these hollow spaces and these vibrations cause the voice to resonate. These resonators amplify the sound that comes up through the vocal cords just as a radio needs speakers. Without these resonators no one would be able to hear the sound you make. The mouth is the most important resonator because it is the largest, all of our sounds come out through it and the movement of the lips and the tongue change the shape of it. To exercise your resonators you need to practice the following sounds: 'n', 'm' and 'ng'. Remember, it's the sounds not the names of the letters that's important. A long humming sound is required. Practice humming now.

Now say the following line with an exaggerated hum on the 'm' and 'n' sounds.

The New York Marathon means I run many miles.

It should sound like this:

The NNNNew York mmmararthonnn mmeanns I runnn mmmanny mmmiles. My mummy made me swim a mile.

MMMy mmummmy mmade mmme swimmm a mmmile.

FACIAL EXPRESSION AND GESTURE

Facial expression is essential in communication. We need to use our eyes, eyebrows and mouths to reinforce what we mean. If we are saying something serious we need to look serious, if we're joking we need to smile. These expressions shouldn't look rehearsed. Don't think, 'oh, this is a serious bit, I must look serious.' If you fully understand and believe in what you're saying your face will show the correct expression at the correct time. Some groups of people need to see our faces more than others – children often need to see our face because they don't always understand the vocabulary we use and the hard of hearing find it helpful, they can try to lip read what we say or just use our general expression to guess what we mean.

Gesture can be used to emphasize a point but mustn't be overdone. A speaker who fidgets and gestures too much is very disconcerting. Gesture is great when you're teaching or explaining but if you're talking to a business person can become very distracting. Imagine hands flying all over the place or a head that nods up and down all the time. It's very difficult in these circumstances to concentrate on what is being said.

All of the above, inflection, pausing, power, pitch, pace, facial expression and gesture are ways of emphasizing specific important words.

You must remember that emphasizing different words can alter the meaning of what you're saying. This can be very important when you're speaking to children.

Reading aloud from your notes or a book

You may have to read aloud from a piece you've never seen before or that you've only had a chance to glance through. When reading aloud in these circumstances there are a few points to make note of.

Hold the piece you're reading so that it doesn't hide your face and also not so low that you end up talking to the floor. Look at your audience on the important words, but try to avoid looking up and down like a yo-yo. If you can't manage to look up without losing your place at least look up at your audience on the first words of each paragraph and end your reading by looking at the audience.

As with any kind of speaking, you need to understand what you're saying. Pick out a few key words which you would like to emphasize. For the moment we'll assume that on these key words you will make eye contact with the audience, so look at them when you say these key words. To avoid speaking too fast, every time you come across a full stop or comma, say 'full stop' or 'comma' to yourself. See the example on page 35

If you're using notes which are only there to jog your memory don't be frightened to look at them but make sure you only write on one side of the card. You can guarantee that when you glance at the notes you'll be reading the wrong side if there's writing on both sides!

Trying to hide the notes and then fumbling around to sneak a glance does not give a very professional impression. Have your notes in front of you, don't fiddle with them, look at them when you need to and don't try to hide them. If you have notes which you want to read from (rather than just to use as reminders), it's helpful to underline the parts you want to look up on. Go through your speech and pick out the important words and underline them. Also make sure that you underline the first sentence and the last sentence.

If you need to have a drink, void cold water, warm water is much better. Dairy products should also be avoided as they cause mucus to form. If you want a drink that will relax your vocal cords try honey and lemon.

National Curriculum/Speech Classes

As part of the National Curriculum in England and Wales, children are assessed on their speaking and listening skills. One of the ways teachers do this is to ask the children to give presentations in front of their classmates. The following pages are written especially for children who have to give a presentation, speech, show and tell or talk at school or college. These pages can be used solely by children, especially older children or you might find it easier if parents and children work together.

The information is written with regard to informative speeches but the basics are the same for any speech or talk

5 STEPS TO PREPARING A SPEECH

1. Choose your topic. Your school may have given you a title or you might have to choose your own. If possible choose a topic you're interested in and if you're stuck for ideas have a look at the list on page?

2. Know what you want to say. If it's a talk for school, write it down first or talk about your topic to your mum or dad and ask them to write down what you're saying in note form. You can then write it out and organize it later.

3. Once you have your talk written down, read it out loud and get someone to see how long it takes you – or time your self with a stop watch. If you've been asked to give a speech at school or college you should have been told how long it needs to be. Make sure when you read your speech out for the first time it takes less time than you've been allowed. For example if the school says 6 mins make sure that on first reading it takes no longer than 5 mins. The more you prepare your speech the longer it will take to say!

4. If you need to use photos or objects in your presentation now is the time to find them. Make sure that you can carry the objects to school safely. If you're using photos or pictures make sure they are big enough for your listeners to see. You might want to enlarge them on your computer.

5. Find out if you're allowed to read your speech, if you need to use just notes or if you have to memorize it.

5 STEPS TO PRACTISING A SPEECH

1. If you're reading your speech to your classmates, practice holding the paper. Make sure that you hold it up high enough so that you're not looking down at the floor but not so high that you hide your face.

2. I always stick (or print) my talk onto card and it's easier to read if it's on A5 paper rather than A4. A4 paper can hide your face very easily so just turn it round (landscape style and print your talk in two columns).

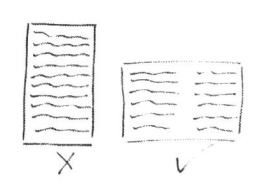

3. Now underline the title and the first and last sentence.

4. Next underline any important words that are in your speech. These are the things that you think your listeners should remember from your talk or anything exciting in your talk. An easy way to pick out the important words is to imagine that you can only hear a few words of your speech – which words would you need to hear to be able to intelligently guess what was being said.

5. Now read your speech out loud and when you get to a word or a sentence that is underlined – look up at your listeners.

OPEN YOUR MOUTH

1. If you want the listeners to hear you, the sound needs to get out of your mouth, so the first thing you need to learn is how to open your mouth wide enough to let the sound get out.

2. When you say a word that has an 'eye' sound in it (such as night, style, kite), you need to be able to put two or three fingers in your mouth – vertically!

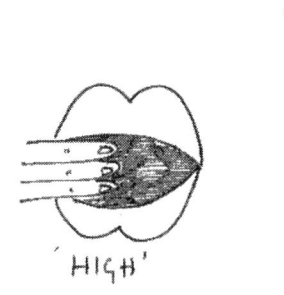

'HIGH'

3. I suggest that you try to get three fingers in your mouth when practicing and two when speaking in public – otherwise you might look a bit daft!

4. The same applies to the 'ah' sound that we find in car, farm, star etc.

5. There are two ways to practice opening your mouth – the first is by saying these sentences out loud:

a) My kite is flying high in the sky

b) My fast car is great for driving to the farm c) A bright light can damage my eye

OR

You can make funny faces in the mirror – see how wide you can open your mouth

3 STEPS TO SLOWING DOWN

1. Most children speak too fast when they get excited or nervous. If you practice your talk you shouldn't be too nervous but you might feel a bit shy about talking in front of other people. One way to slow down is to open your mouth wider (as explained on previously)

2. If you're reading your talk (and this is also great if you have to read aloud from a book in class) an easy way to slow down is to say 'comma' or 'full stop' to yourself every time you see one in your reading.

An example is

An old woman was sweeping her house, (say comma to yourself) **and she found a little crooked sixpence.** (Say full stop to yourself)

'What,' (comma) **said she,** (comma) **'shall I do with this little sixpence?** (question mark) **I will go to market,** (comma) **and buy a little pig.'** (full stop)

You'll find that this simple exercise will slow down your speaking and improve your reading aloud skills more than you thought possible.

3. When you're practicing your talk, every time you come to the end of a paragraph or idea, take a breath. Imagine you're a famous footballer and you've just scored a goal. What would you do?

You'd stop and let the crowd cheer and they'd say to their friends 'what a great goal!'

Then you'd get your breath back and make your way back to your position to restart the match.

You wouldn't score the goal, rush back to position and restart the match in a few seconds!

So why do people speak in that way? You need to get to the end of an idea and then take a breath.

There are 3 reasons for doing this:

1. So that your listeners have a chance to think about what you've said. If you've said something funny they'll have a chance to laugh – make sure you give them time.

2. So that you can take a breath.

3. So that you can get ready for the next thing you want to say. You might want to pick up a photo or object that you need to talk about next.

5 STEPS TO STANDING CORRECTLY

1. When you stand up to say your talk, stand with your feet apart.

2. Let your legs be relaxed, don't straighten your legs so much that your knees lock.

3. Stand up straight but don't stand like a soldier on parade or a gymnast. Soldiers and gymnasts look very smart but they don't have to give a talk at the same time as standing to attention.

4. Keep your head up – you don't want to talk to the floor.

5. A good way to make sure your words go where you want them to is to imagine that your words are like balls. If you wanted to throw a ball to your listeners you would aim it at them not at he floor.

10 TOP TIPS

1. Open your mouth. No one will know how clever you are if they can't hear what you have to say.

2. Be enthusiastic – if you sound excited about your talk your listeners will be excited.

3. Speak slowly and pause after each new thought.

4. If you do go wrong – don't worry. I expect most people listening won't even notice, especially if you ignore it.

5. Practice your talk OUT LOUD.

6. Try to include at least one thing in your talk that your listeners won't already know. Then they'll go away thinking that they've learnt something new from your speech

7. Look at the people you're talking to.

8. If you say 'um' or 'ah' when you can't think of what you want to say next, try to think 'um' or 'ah' instead of saying it.

9. Try not to fidget when you're speaking.

10. If people ask you questions at he end of your talk, make sure you listen carefully. It's a lot easier to answer a question when you've listened to it properly.

TOPICS FOR YOUR TALK

1. How to use a computer

2. How to make a birthday card

3. Why children like Christmas

4. How to stop hiccups

5. Why I like listening to Robbie Williams (or any other singer)

6. How to play monopoly

7. The importance of a healthy diet

8. How to write a letter

9. All about Harry Potter

10. Why it's important to brush our teeth.

11. Why girls like Pink.

12. My Neighbours

13 Things I like

14. Leisure time

15. Dreams and what they mean

16. My Lucky Day

17. Pets as therapy

18. Choosing clothes for other people

19. Grandparents

20. Uninvited guests

21. How to deliver a speech

22. How to bake cookies

23. How to decorate a Christmas Tree

24. History of St John Ambulance

25. How to drive a car

26. Discover Disneyland Paris in two days
27. Understanding Shakespeare
28. The importance of good nutrition
29. The life of Marilyn Monroe
30. Holidaying in..........(your favourite place)
31. The films of Alfred Hitchcock
32. Olympic Gold Medalists
33. The importance of stretching before exercising
34. Why we celebrate Christmas
35. An explanation of the star signs
36. How to make a scarecrow
37. All about Strawberries.
38. Why we shouldn't get sun burnt.
39. Memories
40. How to take a good photograph

POEMS WRITTEN FOR CHILDREN TO READ ALOUD

My Puppy by S.G.

I love my little puppy

With his big brown fluffy ears.

I take him for a walk each day

But all he wants to do is play.

His little legs just run and run

Until it's late and time for bed,

And then we snuggle up together.

He's my best friend and will be forever.

My Football Team by S.G.

Some football teams wear red and white,

They look amazing, what a sight!

But what about their football skills,

Are they boring or full of thrills?

We tackle, shoot, then score a goal,

We look a mess, but we're in control.

Our kit is strange, a cricketers cream.

But do we care? No, we're the winning team.

Teddy Bear by S.G.

My teddy bear sits at the table

And behaves as well as he is able.

He loves to eat a piece of cake,

And gets rid of crumbs by having a shake.

I have to help clear up his mess

Because when asked to work, he's motionless!

Jumping by S.G

I love to jump upon my bed

But mum gets angry, her face goes red.

My bed won't break, I'm only small,

But mum says it's me that'll break if I fall.

Dragon by S.G.

Underneath the castle lives a dragon in the cold.

He's very, very grumpy and very, very old.

He hides away from children who visit just to stare.

And roars a roar so loud, that it gives us all a scare.

He keeps his dungeon hot by breathing out a flame

And if he happens to frighten you, then he's very glad you came.

Sleep by S.G.

When I'm tired I try to sleep,

I close my eyes and dare not peep!

I'd love to be a Pirate by S.G.

A pirate's journey is thrill after thrill

With big strong waves (that make me ill).

The ride is bumpy but they still steer the ship,

Tie knots galore, wash decks, each trip.

Their reward is treasure, money and gold.

That they love to count until they're old.

Yes, I'd love to travel with Captain Nick,

But all that excitement might make me sick.

An Old Lady Remembers by S.G.

An old lady sits by her new garden fence,

She looks at her flowers and thinks it makes sense

To plant some more tulips, where once was a shed.

It was the den of her husband, now sadly dead.

She sits and she smiles as she remembers the past

How she and old Albert would sit on the grass.

They'd picnic on cakes she'd made to save pence.

The money they saved, bought the new garden fence.

VOICE EXERCISES

Vowel Sounds

'a' pronounced 'ah'

F<u>a</u>rmers work very h<u>a</u>rd

My c<u>a</u>r is a f<u>a</u>st motor c<u>a</u>r

'a' pronounced 'ay'

B<u>a</u>bies are too small to pl<u>ay</u> on sk<u>a</u>tes

St<u>ay</u> there J<u>a</u>y

'I' pronounced 'eye'

<u>I</u> tr<u>i</u>ed to b<u>uy</u> a k<u>i</u>te last n<u>i</u>ght

M<u>i</u>ce are t<u>i</u>ny and their noses are <u>shi</u>ny

Consonant sounds

't' and 'd'

I los<u>t</u> my ca<u>t</u>

Comple<u>t</u>e the le<u>tt</u>er an<u>d</u> pu<u>t</u> it in the mi<u>dd</u>le

Chocola<u>t</u>e cake is deligh<u>t</u>ful

Don't be frightened to correct a child every time they miss a 't' or 'd'.

'th'

<u>Th</u>is is my finger

<u>Th</u>is is my <u>th</u>umb

<u>Th</u>e wea<u>th</u>er on my bir<u>th</u>day is often very <u>th</u>undery

To get a good 'th' sound the tongue needs to go between the teeth – look in a mirror to make sure you can see your tongue.

*Remember the tongue has to be between the teeth **before** the sound is made.*

'b' and 'p'

Bread and butter is best for picnics

Put a piece of pie in your pocket

'm'

My mummy made me some marmite toast

Tongue agility

These work the tongue hard

1. Two little toddlers playing table tennis
2. Twenty two players taken out for a treat
3. Fifteen metre tracks are shorter than fifty metre tracks
4. Adults who play table tennis are extremely fit

A good 'ch' and 'J' sound needs a strong tongue and can be achieved by making the tongue touch the top of the mouth before the sound is made.

1. Charlie chews jam biscuits
2. Joe just loves jelly

Resonance

Hum the 'm' and 'n' sounds

1. Now is the time to introduce netball
2. Swimming is fun in the summer months
3. My martial arts instructor always smiles when he wins
4. Mini tennis is fun for small children

Lip agility

1. Betty plays competitive badminton

2. Weightlifters acquire many muscles

3. Boys love to play billiards

4. When I play polo I usually win

BONUS LESSONS

For use with groups of children, if you are talking to only one child alter the sessions to suit you.

Quickly introduce 'Speaking Tot' the soft toy (or any toy) and explain that Speaking Tot will be helping out each lesson. Although Speaking Tot is not written into the lesson plans every lesson, if the children seem to want him, you can easily incorporate him every lesson. Young children often find it easier to talk to a toy.

Lesson 1

Now get your picture cards of three animals, I suggest cat, dog and giraffe but you can substitute your own pictures if you feel you need to.

Show these pictures to the children and discuss each one.

The same method will be used throughout these sessions with different pictures so I will go into more detail here than I will in future lessons.

Teacher: 'Does anyone know what this is?'

Andy: 'A dog'

Teacher: 'Yes, it's a dog. Can anyone tell me how many legs it has?'

Chloe: 'Four'

Teacher: 'That's right. This dog has four legs but can anyone tell me what colour its ears are?'

_____

If the children hesitate, what ever you do don't pressure the children into answering. This has to be fun.

Always repeat the answer in a sentence so that the children get used to hearing sentences.

You must never make them feel embarrassed about being shy.

_____

Answer; 'Black'

Teacher: 'Yes, this dog has four legs and black ears but does it have a tail?'

Steph: 'Yes'

Teacher: 'That's right. This black dog with four legs and black ears has also got a tail.'

Once you have established that the dog has four legs, black ears, is white and black and has a tail you can move on another picture and do the same.

If you haven't time, don't worry. It's better to do one picture well than to rush through all the pictures. There will be sessions where you can go back over some of the previous lessons.

If you have some chatty children encourage them to talk but don't let one or two of the children or parents take over the class.

Lesson 2

Now get your picture cards of two toys, I suggest teddy bear and Buzz Lightyear but you can substitute your own pictures if you feel you need to.

Show these pictures to the children and discuss each one.
The same method will be used as in the first session.

Teacher: 'Does anyone know what this is?'
Andy: 'A teddy'
Teacher: 'Yes, it's a teddy bear. Can anyone tell me what colour it is?'
Chloe: 'Blue'
Teacher: 'That's right. This teddy is blue. How many legs has this teddy got?'
Answer; 'Two'
Teacher: 'Yes, this blue teddy has two legs. Do you think this teddy feels soft?'
Steph: 'Yes'
Teacher: 'That's right. This blue teddy has two legs and feels very soft.'

Now try another card. If you spend too long with one picture the children will get bored.

Teacher: 'Can anyone tell me who this is?'
I would imagine that most children will want to answer so just let them all shout out for now (remember this is only the second session).
'Yes, it's Buzz Lightyear, Scott can you tell me what colour his top is?'
If Scott hesitates and looks worried just got to Chloe.
'Chloe, do you know what colour his top is?'
'Green'
'Yes, Buzz Lightyear has a green top. Does anyone know what he has on his head?'
You might have to get a parent to answer.
'A space helmet'
'Yes, Buzz Lightyear has a space helmet and a green top.'

Carry on until the end of the session.

Remember, if you haven't time, don't worry. It's better to do one picture well than to rush through all the pictures. There will be sessions where you can go back over some of the previous lessons.

Lesson 3

Today the children are going to use their listening skills. Explain that you are going to read a very short story out loud and that when you've finished you will ask some questions.

Make sure you read out the title of the story.

Pirate Treasure

Captain Doug and Pirate Princess Steph loved looking for treasure and their favourite treasure was gold coins. Captain Doug had a new treasure map and so Pirate Princess Steph and Captain Doug started to look for more treasure. Captain Doug had to walk five paces from the tree. Now Captain Doug's legs were very long so his footsteps were very big and Pirate Princess Steph was tiny so her footsteps were very small. So while Captain Doug walked his five steps, Pirate Princess Steph had to take twelve footsteps to keep up with him.

Captain Doug then had to dig a hole to find the treasure. Luckily he had long arms as well as long legs so he could reach into the hole very easily.

Both Captain Doug and Pirate Princess Steph were expecting to find gold but they had a huge surprise – Captain Doug found a very large chest in the hole and when they opened it they found it was full of ……. What do you think? …tea!

Luckily Captain Doug and Pirate Princess Steph weren't too upset because tea was their favourite drink.

They closed the chest and carried it very carefully back to their ship, which was called the 'flying fish' and they made themselves a nice cup of tea.

If the children are very young you might want to read it again before you ask the questions.

Ask the children the following questions

1. What was the story called?
2. What was the Captains name?
3. What was the Pirate Princess called?

4. What did Captain Doug have?
5. What did they like finding?
6. How many steps did Captain Doug have to take?
7. How many steps did Pirate Princess Steph have to take?
8. Did Captain Doug have long or short legs?
9. What did they find in the chest?
10. What was their ship called?

Lesson 4

Find some pictures that represent Winter, Autumn, Summer and Spring.

In case you run out of time I suggest that you start with Summer and Winter.

Show the summer and winter cards and establish what the seasons are.

'Chloe, do you know when this picture was taken?'
'The winter'
'Yes, this is the winter – how do we know it's winter?'
'Because of the snow'
'Yes, there's snow on the ground so is it hot or cold in the winter Tony?'
'Cold'
'Yes, it's cold in the winter.'

Do the same with the other cards.

If the children are too young to understand the seasons concentrate on hot and cold.

Lesson 5

Explain that today you are all going to talk about parts of our body, especially ears, eyes, nose, mouth and hands.

Ask:

"What do we do with our ears?"

"Hear"

'Yes, that's right, we can hear things with our ears what do we do with our eyes?'

'We look'

'Yes, we see with our eyes. Chloe what do we do with our eyes, we........'

'Adam, what can you do with your nose?'

'Sniff'

'Yes, we can sniff with our nose but we also use it to do something else. Does anyone know what it is?'

If no one answers, ask one of the mums if they can tell the children.

'We smell'

'Yes we smell with our nose and we see with our ………and we listen with our........'

'What do we do with out mouth?'

'Talk'

'Yes, we can talk with our mouths. What else do we use our mouth for?'

'Food'

'Good Tony, we use our mouth to taste our food'

'Now this is an easy one, what do we use our hands for?'

'Everything'

'Yes it seems like it doesn't it? If you wanted to know how cold a piece of snow was, what would you do?'

'Touch it'

'Yes, that's right, you'd use your hands to touch it.'

'Ann what would you use to hear a dog barking?'

'I'd use my ears'

'Yes, we'd use our ears to hear the dog'

Lesson 6

Today we are going to concentrate on articulation and how sounds are made in the mouth.
We are going to use tongue twisters and short rhymes.

'th' sound – you must use tongue and teeth.
You can encourage young children to stick their tongue out to get the correct sound.

'This is my finger,
This is my thumb'

The 'f' sound should use teeth and lip

'Thirty thick pieces of fudge'

End consonants – point out to mums that quite often the only sound that differentiates words is the final consonant.

An example is bed, bet, beg, ben.
If children leave off the final sound all the words will sound the same.

Use other examples, cod, cot. Con. Cog

Vowel sounds.

Explain that for the vowel sound to come out the mouth must be open.
All of the **'eye' sounds** should be said with your mouth wide open

'I fly my kite at night'

Consonant sounds

Betty bought a bit of butter

Thirty thousand thimbles

Use as many tongue twisters as you like

Lesson 7

Today we want the children to try and describe something to us, but remember if you have ten children in your group, by the time they've all settled, played the name game and understood what you're talking about you're only going to have about 20 mins left - that's only 2 mins per child. You might want to split them into groups.

1. What does a car look like?
2. What does a tree look like?
3. What does a baby look like?
4. What does a dog look like?
5. What does a shop look like?
6. What does a cup look like?
7. What does a train look like?
8. What does a bus look like?
9. What does a television look like?
10. What does a chair look like?

Choose items that the children are familiar with – this will depend on the age of the child and the area they live in.

Lesson 8

Today we're going to talk about days of the week.
Ask the children if they know what day of the week it is.
Discuss the fact that there are 7 days in a week.
Say them out loud and get the children to repeat them after you.

Ask if the children do anything special on different day.

Examples

Always visit Grandma on Sunday
Go swimming on Tuesdays
Have a certain meal on a Wednesday
Big sister goes to Brownies on Saturday

Always repeat the answer in a sentence and quickly carry on to the next question.

Lesson 9

Ask the children what you call the thing that you:

1. Use to talk to people – phone
2. Use to put drink in – cup/bottle
3. Use to unlock a door – key
4. Use to cut our food up with – knife
5. Use to dry ourselves with – towel
6. Put on your feet – shoes/boots/slippers
7. go to sleep in at night – bed
8. cook your food on – cooker
9. put your shopping in – trolley/bag/car
10. clean your teeth with - brush/toothpaste

When the children answer repeat it,

For example

'key'

'Yes we use a key to unlock a door'

You could then ask what else we unlock with a key.

The answers could include case, safe, diary, car.

Lesson 10

Today we are going to introduce poetry

Ask if any of the children know what a poem is?
Some of the answers might include nursery rhyme, song, story, words.

Explain that it like a nursery rhyme but that you say it rather than sing it. Explain that a poem can be very long or very short.

Remind them of Teddy Bear

Teddy Bear sat on a chair
With Ham and Jam and Plum and Pear.
This is strange said Teddy Bear,
'The more I eat, the less is there.'

Read another poem to the children

Dragon by S.G.

Underneath the castle lives a dragon in the cold.
He's very, very grumpy and very, very old.
He hides away from children who visit just to stare.
And roars a roar so loud, that it gives us all a scare.
He keeps his dungeon hot by breathing out a flame
And if he happens to frighten you, then he's very glad you came.

Ask
  1. Who lived beneath the castle?
  2. Who does he hide from?
  3. What noise does he make?

4. Is he very old or very young?
5. What does he breathe out?
6. Do the children like him?
7. What do the children do when they see him?

Below is a very short poem the children can learn.

Sleep by S.G.

When I'm tired I try to sleep
I close my eyes and dare not peep

Lesson 11

This week we're going to get the children to say some nursery rhymes.

I've chosen

Jack and Jill

The Grand Old Duke of York

Humpty Dumpty

However, these may not be popular nursery rhymes where you live so change them if you need to.

Once you've all recited one of the rhymes try to encourage the children to retell the story in their own words.

Jack and Jill went up a hill

To fetch a pale of water

Jack fell down and broke his crown

And Jill came tumbling after.

If the children have difficulty retelling the rhyme encourage them with questions:

1. What did Jack and Jill climb up?
2. What did they want to get?
3. Who fell down?
4. What did Jill do?

Remember to repeat the answer in a sentence each time.

The Grand Old Duke of York

He had ten thousand men

He marched them up to the top of the hill

And he marched them down again.

When they were up they were up

And when they were down they were down
And when they were only half way up
They were neither up nor down.

Humpty Dumpty sat on a wall
Humpty Dumpty had a great fall
All the Kings horses
And all the Kings men
Couldn't put Dumpty together again.

Lesson 12

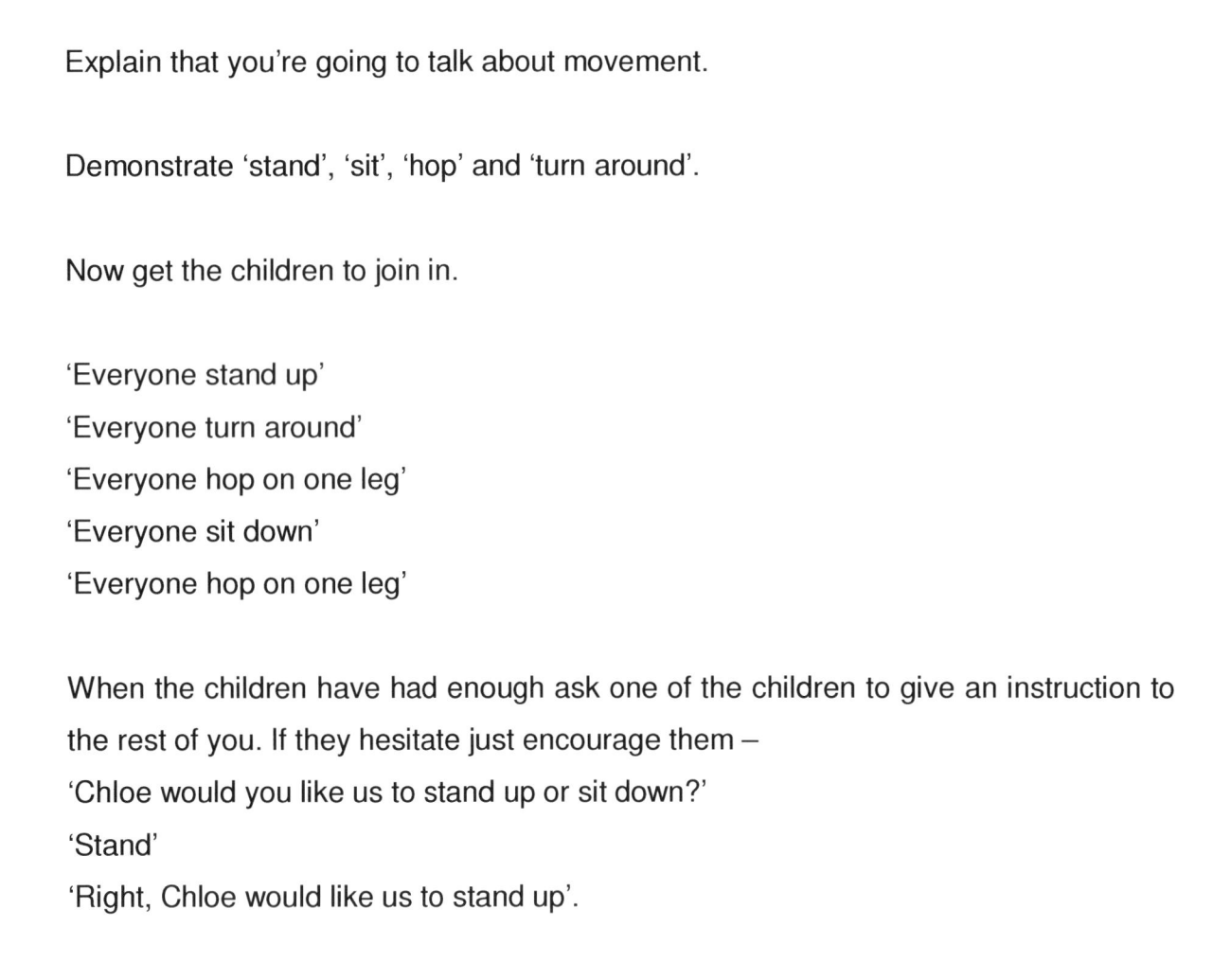

Today we're going to concentrate on stand, sit, turn around and hop.

Explain that you're going to talk about movement.

Demonstrate 'stand', 'sit', 'hop' and 'turn around'.

Now get the children to join in.

'Everyone stand up'
'Everyone turn around'
'Everyone hop on one leg'
'Everyone sit down'
'Everyone hop on one leg'

When the children have had enough ask one of the children to give an instruction to the rest of you. If they hesitate just encourage them –
'Chloe would you like us to stand up or sit down?'
'Stand'
'Right, Chloe would like us to stand up'.

Then ask another child.

Lessons for older children

LESSON 1

Describing places

Split the group into teams if it is a large group. Each person should think of one part of the town (or area) in which they live.

Ask each team to give a short speech of a minute and a half telling the more important facts about the area. Tell the children not to change their speech just because someone else does the same area.

Here is an example:

'I live in Primrose Way. This is part of a small estate of houses. We have a bus once an hour into the main town. About a two minute walk away is a supermarket, a small library, the village hall and a playground. This village has 2 first schools and a middle school, a doctors surgery, a petrol station, a vet, four churches, two post offices, hairdressers, a fish and chip shop and lots of open spaces. Most of the houses and bungalows have nice gardens and although we live in the country we can get to Bournemouth in about 40 mins.'

Once they have all spoken (or one member from each team) discuss if they would rather live in a town or the country? Get them to give reasons. Ask them where they would suggest a visitor to the area would stay and visit.

The first time the children try this they may just give a list of amenities, however with your help they should be able to include:

Description of area,

Distance from town, country, from the sea or river etc.

How to travel to other places

Local shops, parks, schools, churches

Type of people who live in the area, young, old, families.

You could give this outline at the beginning of the lesson if you wish.

LESSON 2

This game will help everyone's articulation.

Ask a pupil to say any word that comes into their head. Imagine the word is 'speaking'. Now ask the child sitting next (or opposite) to say a word that begins with the last letter of that word – ' Glorious'. Now the next - 'Sugar'. If the same letter comes up (and e is very popular) the child has to say a word that hasn't been said.

This game has a few variations. This time after the child has said the word they have to put it in a sentence. So for speaking they could say:
Speaking – I like speaking at home
Glorious – The weather was glorious yesterday
Sugar – I try not to eat too much sugar because it will make me overweight.

You could play the game where every answer has to be a person's name, or a place or an animal.

The game could be played in teams as a competition so the children would try very hard to pick words with difficult final letters.

To get the children interested in articulation you could ask them the reasons why some people may not be able to understand some of the words. Perhaps the ends of the words aren't being said clearly, or the words are too quiet, or too quick. The vowel sounds might need to be said more openly.

Once children have tired of this game (I've found they love to play this for ages!) you could find some pictures from magazines or photos of the area etc and ask the children in turn to describe one thing in the picture without saying what it is and the others have to guess. This can be done at the end of any lesson with any picture and will help children put their thoughts into words. If they say 'it's red', remind them that they should say 'the object I'm describing is red' if no one guesses they carry on – 'the object is very tiny and red'

The more detailed the picture is the more fun and more challenging this becomes. Pictures like the ones used in the 'Where's Wally' books are ideal.

LESSON 3

Find a nursery rhyme or poem that all the children know. (If this isn't possible it can be done using lists – see later).
Song lyrics would be alright or a nursery rhyme that children can remember from when they were young.

One person says the first line, then the teacher (or another appointed child) points to another member of the class and they must continue the next line, then point to another child etc. Go quickly form one child to another. Encourage clear speech so that the other children know where they are in the rhyme. You can go back to a child who has already said a line.
This lesson helps with memory and articulation.

This word game can also be played using lists. Ask for names of trees and each child has to answer within 5 seconds. You make it competitive by awarding points and taking points away if the children hesitate too much.

Lists that can be used include,
Films, Countries, flowers, street names etc.

If you have a large group you could split the group into two and give each team a different poem or rhyme. They can then take it in turns to say a line.

Towards the end of the lessons you could find some pictures from magazines or photos of the area etc and ask the children in turn to describe one thing in the picture without saying what it is and the others have to guess. This can be done at the end of any lesson with any picture and will help children put their thoughts into words. If they say 'it's red', remind them that they should say 'the object I'm describing is red' if no one guesses they carry on – 'the object is very tiny and red'

The more detailed the picture is the more fun and more challenging this becomes. Pictures like the ones used in the 'Where's Wally' books are ideal.

LESSON 4

This lesson helps children to understand how sounds are made in the mouth.

Ask questions that require a specific word or words to be in the answer.
For example, ask the children for three words that end in 'p'.
Answers could be 'Hemp. Lump. Imp'.
The answer will be wrong if it doesn't end in a 'p' or if the final 'p' is not sounded.

You could ask for words to be put into complete sentences. Naturally you will choose words that your class may find difficult to pronounce.

Three words with the 't' sound in the middle might produce – bottle, water, rotten.

Ask for words ending in p, t, k, b, d, g, or ng.
Ask for words the begin with 'th'
Ask for words that rhyme with 'light' 'oil' or 'shout'

This lesson gives you a great opportunity to explain to older children how different sounds are made in the mouth.
'th' uses tongue and teeth
'b' uses both lips
'f' uses teeth and lips
't' uses tongue and hard palate

Choose sounds that your class have difficulty with. Quite young children can understand how these sounds are made and older children might be interested in how they are classified – labiels, labiodentals etc.

Towards the end of the lessons you could find some pictures from magazines or photos of the area etc and ask the children in turn to describe one thing in the picture without saying what it is and the others have to guess. This can be done at the end of any lesson with any picture and will help children put their thoughts into words. If they say 'it's red', remind them that they should say 'the object I'm describing is red' if no one guesses they carry on – 'the object is very tiny and red'

The more detailed the picture is the more fun and more challenging this becomes. Pictures like the ones used in the 'Where's Wally' books are ideal.

LESSON 5

This lesson aims at clear, thoughtful sentences.

Explain to the children that you're going to ask them to describe an event or an object so that other people can recognise it at once.
Also explain that you don't want sentences such as 'we,, it was sort of – you know – all over the place, you know what I mean, don't you'

Try objects first. The teacher can do the first one to show the children what to do. Imagine you have a table and describe it to the class without saying what it is. Can they guess what you're talking about?

Here a re a few easy examples to try.

Box	Mobile phone	Chair
Bottle	Knife	Bag
Plate	Bowl	Saucepan
Cup	Comb	

Try to get the children to be exact.
'A flat round object made of china' might be a plate or a saucer.

'My object has a handle and attached to it are a number of prongs ' is supposed to describe a table fork but it could also be comb or a garden fork used for digging.

What is the object made of? How long is the handle? How big is the whole object?

More difficult objects could include Kettle, Shoe, Desk

LESSON 6

This lesson concentrates on conversation.

Most people find it easy to talk when they are with friends and family but if you ask them to speak at a specific time they will panic. However people generally chat quite easily if they're in a queue.

If you have 2 or more children in your group, they can work in pairs. If you have only one you will have to converse with the child.

Write the following types of queues on to pieces of paper (one on each piece). Let one of the children pick a piece of paper at random.

<u>Types of Queues</u>

Queuing for the cinema
Bus Queue
Queuing for concert tickets
Queuing for railway tickets
Queuing in a shop
Queuing for a football match

Add any other queues that are relevant to your class.

Chat as though you are in the queue.
What type of concert?
Have you seen them before?
Is the railway journey long or short?
What are you buying in the shop?

Don't expect too much from the children. Encourage articulation but don't worry too much about grammar to start with.

Once the children are at ease talking you can insist that they speak in sentences.

LESSON 7

The aim of this lesson is to achieve a clear statement and distinct speech, while giving simple answers.

Below is a list of events.

A puncture on the way home

The washing line breaks

You miss the last bus

You leave a parcel on the train

Your hat blows into the sea

You drop your camera in the swimming pool

You fall over in front of a lot of people

There are 2 ways to play this game.

If you have the facilities, ask a volunteer to go out of the room. The rest of the class choose one of the above events.

When the volunteer comes back into the room he has to ask each child in turn, 'What would you do?'

The children in turn give a one sentence answer but they mustn't repeat an answer already given.

Example – Answers to 'A puncture on the way home' might be

I would start walking

I would push the machine

I would go for help

I would try to mend it myself.

Eventually some one will guess the predicament.

If you don't have facilities for the person to leave the room or only have a very small group, you can print the events on to pieces of paper. Let a child (or teacher) pick a piece and then see if the other child can guess in less than 10 answers.

LESSON 8

In this lesson children learn how to put certain words into either sentences or paragraphs.

Choose words suitable for the age of your group, making sure that they are not too easy.

You could ask other members of the class to suggest words.

If your class find it very easy to put the word into a sentence, give them a list of words to put into a paragraph.

Try to discourage hesitation such as 'um' or 'you know'

Some suggested words or group of words are below

Authority
Pompous
Specialise
Extraordinary
Effective

Seaweed, sand, rock, pier, waves
Books, paper, ink
Bat, umpire, over, ball
Car, policeman, fast

You could make your groups of unrelated words to make the task more challenging.

LESSON 9

For this lesson ask everyone to bring in an object from home they can talk about.

This could be anything (preferably quite small) such as a toy teddy, favourite trainers, magazine etc.

Ask the children to talk about their object with no preparation for 1 minute! Most people run out of things to say after 30 seconds. Tell them not to worry - you can stop them when they run out of ideas or help them with the talk.

Explain the need to pause between each thought – the slower they speak the less they'll have to say.

Once they've all had a go ask if anyone would like to try and talk for 1 minute about somebody else's object.

Finally ask them once again to talk about their own object.

Hopefully they will now find this a lot easier.

If children find this difficult help them by suggesting they start with:

What the object is

Where they got it from

How long they've had it

Why they like it

Does it have a purpose?

Where they keep it

All they need is to talk for 10 seconds on each point

For your own notes, tongue twisters etc

Printed in Great Britain
by Amazon